Celebration Press Reading

Good Habits
Great Readers™

Student Reader · Volume 1

CELEBRATION PRESS
Pearson Learning Group

Art and Design: Stephen Barth, Tricia Battipede, Alison O'Brien

Editorial: Adam Berkin, Linda Dorf, Alia Lesser, Cynthia Levinson, Linette Mathewson, Jennifer Van Der Heide

Inventory: Yvette Higgins

Marketing: Gina Konopinski-Jacobia

Production/Manufacturing: Lawrence Berkowitz, Alan Dalgleish, Karen Edmonds

Cover Illustrator: Lee White

Celebration Press Reading: Good Habits, Great Readers™

ISBN 1-4284-0436-8

Printed in the United States of America

10   V054   10

Celebration Press
Pearson Learning Group

1-800-321-3106
www.pearsonlearning.com
www.goodhabitsgreatreaders.com

Contents

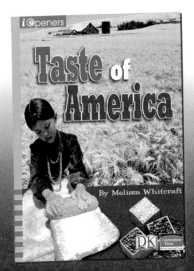

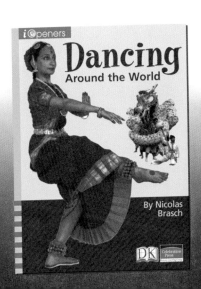

Unit 3 Great Readers Use What They Know

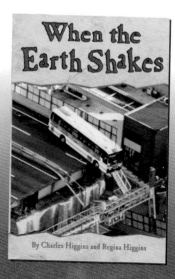

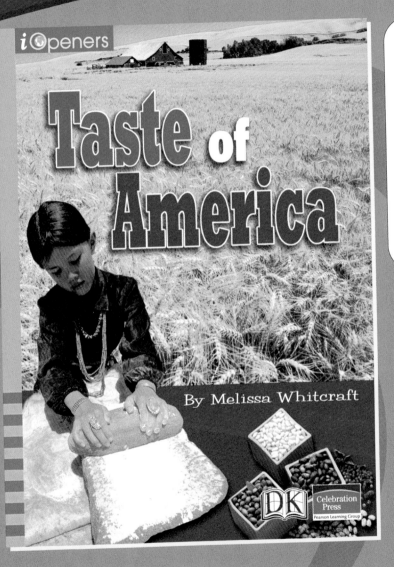

Words to Know

citrus (p. 10): "any fruit of the family that includes oranges, lemons, limes, and grapefruit"

climate (p. 10): "the typical weather conditions in an area"

coast (p. 10): "land along the sea"

Apply the Strategy

Lesson 1

Activating Prior Knowledge to Make Predictions

1. Look at the cover on page 6, the contents page on page 8, and the map on page 9. Use the pages along with your prior knowledge to make predictions about the book.
2. Record your predictions in a T-chart, labeling the left side *Prior Knowledge* and the right side *My Predictions.*

Prior Knowledge	My Predictions

Lesson 2

Using Text Structure to Make Predictions

1. Read pages 9–11. Look through pages 16–24, and use text structure to predict what kind of information you might find in this part of the book.
2. Record your predictions on a concept web.

3. Read pages 16–24 to confirm or revise your predictions.

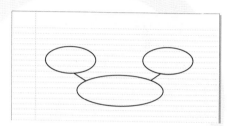

Lesson 3

Using Text Features to Make Predictions

1. Look through pages 25–29. Use the text features to make predictions.
2. Record your predictions in a T-chart, labeling the left side *Text Features* and the right side *My Predictions.*

Text Features	My Predictions

Contents

Foods Around Us

Most supermarkets in the United States offer foods from all around the world. You can buy Mexican taco dinners, Italian spaghetti, and Chinese vegetables. German rye bread or African black-eyed peas are also available. These foods and many others show the different **ethnicities** of the American people.

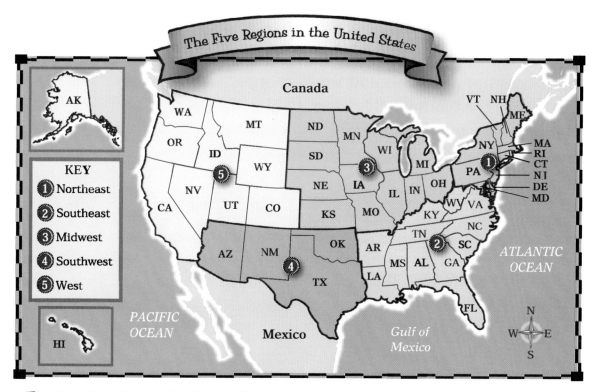

The Five Regions in the United States

KEY
1 Northeast
2 Southeast
3 Midwest
4 Southwest
5 West

Canada

PACIFIC OCEAN

Mexico

Gulf of Mexico

ATLANTIC OCEAN

This book has divided the United States into five regions.

Supermarkets also sell foods that are **indigenous** to the different regions that make up the United States. Indigenous foods come from plants or animals found in a particular geographic area. The climate and land affect the kinds of foods in a region. For example, the rich farmland in the Midwest is good for growing corn. The warm, sunny climate of the south is good for growing citrus fruits.

The location of a region also affects the types of foods found there. For example, regions near the coast depend on the seas for food. That's why fish and shellfish are popular in the Northeast, Southeast, and West regions. Indigenous foods were the main food sources for Native Americans long ago.

Food Facts

As American as apple pie is today, apples are not native to North America. The first trees were brought to New England by Pilgrim settlers from England.

Crabs are plentiful in the waters located in and near the Northeast and Southeast regions.

People from England began to settle in the United States in the 1600s. European settlers followed in the 1800s. Later, people from around the world settled in the United States. All these **immigrants** brought food and recipes from their native countries. They added the foods of the area to their cooking. Today most dishes are a mix of indigenous and **imported** foods. They are also made with recipes and cooking styles from around the world.

Between 1880 and 1930 more than 22 million people from Europe immigrated to the United States.

Indian Pudding

The Native Americans taught the settlers how to make a pudding using **cornmeal**. The settlers added molasses and sugar, which they had brought from their native countries. These ingredients made the pudding sweet. It became known as Indian Pudding. The pudding is still served today, often with sliced apples.

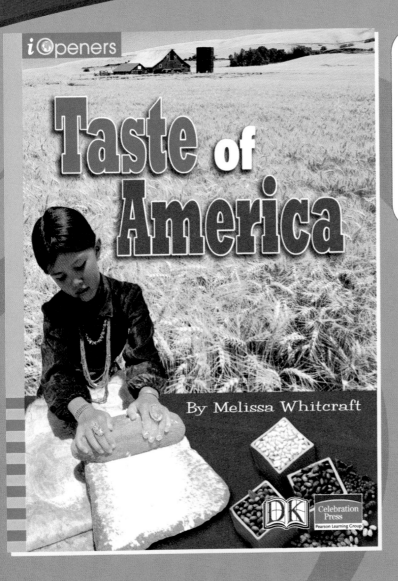

Words to Know

bland (p. 17): "tasteless"

chowder (p. 18): "a thick soup or stew"

grated (p. 20): "made into small pieces by rubbing against something rough"

Apply the Strategy

Lesson 1

Asking Text-Explicit Questions

1. Reread pages 16–20, and think of text-explicit questions.
2. Record questions and answers on a T-chart, labeling the left side *Text-Explicit Questions* and the right side *Answers*.

Text-Explicit Questions	Answers

Lesson 2

Asking Text-Implicit Questions

1. Skim pages 16–20, and think of text-implicit questions. Use clues from the text and your own knowledge and experience to answer the questions.
2. Record your questions, clues, and answers in a three-column chart, labeling the columns *Text-Implicit Questions*, *Clues and Prior Knowledge*, and *Answers*.

Text-Implicit Questions	Clues and Prior Knowledge	Answers

Lesson 3

Generating Questions Throughout Reading

1. Reread pages 21–24, and think of text-explicit and text-implicit questions.
2. Record your questions, clues for text-implicit questions, and answers in a three-column chart, labeling the columns *Questions*, *Clues*, and *Answers*.

Questions	Clues	Answers

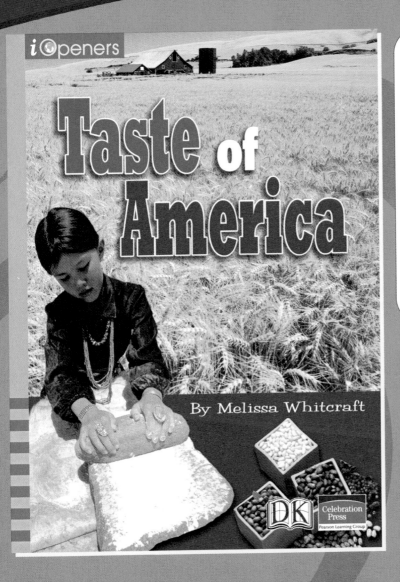

Words to Know

combine (p. 29): "to mix together"

lentils (p. 25): "seeds that may be used in soups or stews"

grazing (p. 27): "feeding on growing grass or herbs"

pharmacist (p. 26): "a person who is trained to prepare and give out medicine"

Apply the Strategy

Lesson 1

Generating Questions to Anticipate Events or Information

1. Read pages 25–29. Pause after pages 25 and 27 to ask questions that the text has made you wonder about.
2. Record your questions in a T-chart, labeling the left side *My Questions* and the right side *Predictions/ Answers*.

My Questions	Predictions/Answers

Lesson 2

Questioning the Author

1. Skim pages 25–29. Think of questions you would like to ask the author.
2. Record questions and possible responses in a T-chart, labeling the left side *Questions to the Author* and the right side *Possible Author Responses*.

Questions to the Author	Possible Author Responses

Lesson 3

Asking Questions to Resolve Confusion

1. Skim pages 25–29.
2. Record questions about things that confuse you in a T-chart, labeling the left side *Questions* and the right side *Solutions*.
3. Work with a partner to resolve the confusions and add solutions to your chart.

Questions	Solutions

The Northeast

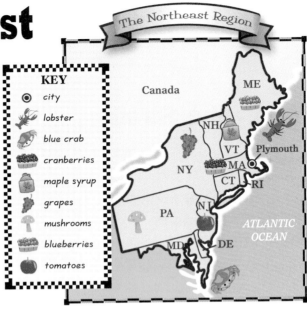

The Northeast Region

KEY
- ⊙ city
- lobster
- blue crab
- cranberries
- maple syrup
- grapes
- mushrooms
- blueberries
- tomatoes

Canada

ME

NH

VT

Plymouth

NY

MA

CT

RI

PA

N.J.

ATLANTIC OCEAN

MD

DE

The Wampanoag (wahm-puh-NOH-ahg) were the first Native American people to live in the Northeast region. They survived by using handmade tools to hunt, fish, and farm. Wild animals, fish, berries, and nuts were indigenous to the Northeast. The Wampanoag planted corn, sweet potatoes, squash, and beans as other sources of food. They also discovered a way to **preserve** the fish they caught.

The Pilgrims arrived from England in 1620. They settled in Plymouth, Massachusetts. The Wampanoag taught the Pilgrims how to hunt, fish, and farm. They also showed them how to tap maple syrup from local trees.

The Wampanoag showed the Pilgrims where wild berries and nuts grew.

In the fall of 1621, the Pilgrims and Native Americans celebrated the first Thanksgiving.

The food the Pilgrims ate was very bland at first. They slowly added new foods and spices to their cooking. These ingredients added more flavor.

One favorite Pilgrim dish was baked beans. The Wampanoag introduced cooked beans to the Pilgrims. They simply cooked the beans in water over a low fire. Then the Pilgrims added salted pork and molasses. This dish is known today as Boston Baked Beans. It is often served with Boston Brown Bread, another dish first made by Pilgrims. This moist bread is made from flour, molasses, and raisins.

Molasses is thick, sweet syrup that settlers imported to add flavor to foods.

Thousands of Irish immigrants came to Boston in the mid-1840s. The potato crop in Ireland failed and farmers had no way to make a living. They had to leave Ireland or starve. The Irish used potatoes in many of their dishes. They added potatoes to the seafood and corn chowders when they arrived. Today, potatoes are one of the main ingredients in any **New England** chowder.

New England is known for its fresh seafood and chowders because of the variety of fish found in its coastal waters.

Lobster and potatoes are the two main ingredients in lobster chowder.

Italian immigrants settled in Boston in the 1880s. They added olive oil, tomatoes, green peppers, and garlic to the fish stews. These Italian ingredients changed the flavor of New England chowders yet again.

Italian immigrants also made pasta popular in the United States. Traditionally most Italians ate pasta with a little olive oil, cheese, and pepper. Italians started eating pasta with tomato sauce in the mid-1800s. Italian restaurants served meat with spaghetti in the United States. This pleased Americans who liked eating meat with their meals. That's how the Italian-American dish, spaghetti and meatballs, was created.

Pasta Takes Shape

The history of pasta goes back thousands of years. The earliest pasta was usually rolled into a long, flat form like lasagna. Beginning in the nineteenth century, new shapes and sizes of pasta could be made by machine. Thomas Jefferson brought the first pasta machine from Europe to the United States.

Italians also brought pizza to the United States. Pizza had been eaten in Italy for hundreds of years. The first pizzas in America were simple. They were made with dough, tomato sauce, and the herbs oregano and basil. The pizzas were also sprinkled with grated Italian cheese. Today, Americans can get almost any type of pizza they want. There is pizza with three cheeses or pizza with no cheese. Pizzas also come with a choice of toppings, including meat and vegetables.

Food Facts

About 3 billion pizzas are sold in the United States each year.

Pizza makes a quick and healthy meal.

The Southeast

The Native Americans in the Southeast survived on berries, nuts, wild animals, and seafood. They also planted peas, squash, onions, corn, and some fruit. Immigrants arrived to the Southeast and planted new crops and began raising animals for food.

English **colonists** settled in the Southeast in the early 1600s. They built large **plantations**. Enslaved Africans were the plantation cooks until slavery was ended in 1865. They prepared several dishes, including collard greens, **succotash**, and hominy. Hominy came from a local Native American custom. They cooked corn kernels until they were soft. Plantation cooks added milk, cream, eggs, and butter.

The Southeast Region

KEY
⊙ city
peanuts and pecans
peaches
shrimp
blue crab
rice
citrus
fish

Since the Spanish brought orange trees to Florida in the early 1500s, Florida has become the main producer of oranges.

Enslaved Africans prepared a variety of dishes in plantation kitchens, like the one above.

African cooks also used black-eyed peas they had brought from Africa. They added local rice and salted pork to create a dish called Hoppin-Jack. This dish is still popular in the Southeast today.

fried chicken

Smoked ham was also served on plantations. Before refrigeration, ham was smoked to keep it from spoiling. Today, smoked ham is often the centerpiece at holiday dinners.

Fried chicken was another popular dish in the Southeast in the nineteenth century. Often the chicken was served with hot biscuits. Today southern fried chicken is served in homes and restaurants everywhere.

The French first settled in New Orleans, Louisiana, in 1718. New Orleans became Spanish when Spain took over the city in 1764. The French and Spanish settlers created another southeastern **cuisine**.

Creole cooking became popular with wealthy French and Spanish traders who lived in New Orleans. The spicy mix of ingredients included local meat and seafood. Spanish green peppers and tomatoes were used for seasoning. The sauces were French. An African vegetable called okra was used to thicken Creole sauces.

A New Orleans restaurant owner holds a plate of Cajun food.

Cajun cooking is similar to Creole cooking. Cajun food was developed by the French colonists known as Acadians. They left Canada and settled on the Mississippi River near New Orleans in 1775.

Cajun cooks also used local meat and seafood in their cooking. They added homegrown onions, rice, and hot peppers for flavor. Their one-pot meals made the most of what the land offered. Cajun and Creole dishes are popular today in restaurants across the United States.

Food Facts

In 1920, automobile inventor Henry Ford invented the charcoal briquette for barbecuing.

Southern Barbecue

When we think of southern food, we can't forget the barbecue, which is thought to have started in the South. True barbecuing is the process of cooking meat at a low temperature for a long time over wood coals. Today, when most Americans barbecue they are actually cooking food over a grill heated by charcoal or gas.

The Southwest

The Pueblo Native Americans of the Southwest survived on the indigenous foods of the region. They hunted wild turkey and other animals. The Pueblos also planted crops, such as pinto beans, squash, and corn that could survive in the hot, dry climate. The corn had long roots which reached down to the damp soil below the surface.

The Spanish arrived to the Southwest in the 1540s. They introduced many of their own crops to the region. They grew oranges, limes, onions, carrots, eggplants, and lentils. The Spaniards used **irrigation** techniques first used by the Pueblos.

The Southwest Region

AZ   NM   OK
      TX
      Mexico

KEY

beef cattle

prickly pear fruit

hot peppers

wheat

watermelons

lettuce

yellow onion

lentils

eggplant

The Spanish brought other foods to the Southwest. Hot peppers were carried from the Aztecs in South America and tortillas from Mexico. The Spanish also brought different animals, such as pigs, goats, and chickens. These animals were raised for their meats. Goats also provided milk for the Spaniards to make cheese.

All these different ingredients were blended together over time. Spanish cooks mixed Native American pinto beans with meat to make *chili con carne*. They also rolled and filled *tortillas* with grated cheese, onion, and meat. This dish is called *enchiladas*. The Spaniards added hot pepper sauce to their foods for spice.

Food Facts

A pharmacist named Colville invented a scale in 1912 to measure the heat in peppers. Today, a more modern scale is used with a rating of zero to ten.

Flattened

The Spanish brought *tortillas*, or "little cakes," from a Native American nation in Mexico. They were made from flattened corn paste. *Tortillas* were flat and soft bread that were also used as spoons or plates.

In the nineteenth century, cowboys moved herds of up to 3,000 cattle north at any one time.

The Spanish also introduced cattle to the Southwest. The dry land was perfect for grazing animals. The Spanish built farms and raised cattle for their beef. They rode around their large ranches on horses they had brought from Spain.

American pioneers from the East started building cattle ranches by the mid-1880s. Cowboys moved the cattle north to be sold during each spring. They rode horses to drive, or move, the cattle along. Sometimes they traveled more than 700 miles on a cattle drive. The length of the trip changed depending on the weather. A drive could take anywhere from twenty-five to one hundred days.

Moving the cattle north was difficult work. Cowboys traveled with a cook and a food wagon called a chuck wagon. The cooks prepared meals for the cowboys. They often didn't have fresh foods because they were out on the trail for so long.

Chuck wagon beans were popular while on the trail. Cooks made this dish by cooking pinto beans with onions, garlic, and salt pork. Chuck wagon beans were served over biscuits with a sprinkle of hot pepper powder for flavor. Cooks also made fajitas. This dish was made from strips of barbecued beef or other meat.

The chuck wagon was filled with enough cooking equipment and supplies to last the length of the cattle drive.

Dried Meat Snack

The cowboys ate dried, smoked strips of beef while out on the trail. They learned this from the Sioux who carried dried, smoked buffalo meat on their hunts. The Spanish called these strips *charqui*. Today, we know this snack as beef jerky.

beef
fajita

Today, many of
these southwestern
cowboy dishes are described as Tex-Mex. These foods
combine flavors and ingredients popular in both Texas
and Mexico. Some dishes are made with a mix of
beans and peppers. Other dishes are a mix of
shredded meats served with corn *tortillas*. Many
southwestern dishes show how Mexican, Spanish,
and pioneer foods blend together.

jalapeño pepper

*A variety of sauces are used to add flavor
to Southwestern Barbecue.*

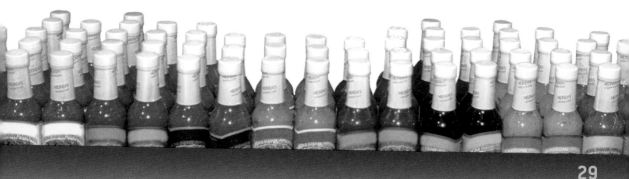

Glossary

colonists   people who settle a colony, or region, in a new country while keeping ties with their native countries

cornmeal   grains of coarsely ground corn

cuisine   style of cooking or preparing of food

ethnicities   characteristics that groups of people share, such as country of origin and culture

immigrants   people who settle in a new country

imported   something brought into one country from another

indigenous   occurring naturally in a particular region; that which is native to an area

irrigation   the process of bringing water to an area such as a field to help crops grow

missions   religious communities

New England   the six northeast states, including ME, VT, NH, MA, RI, and CT

pioneer   having to do with people who were first to settle in a new area

plantations   large southern farms that grew cash crops, such as cotton or tobacco, for profit

preserve   to keep or save from spoiling

succotash   a dish consisting of corn and lima beans

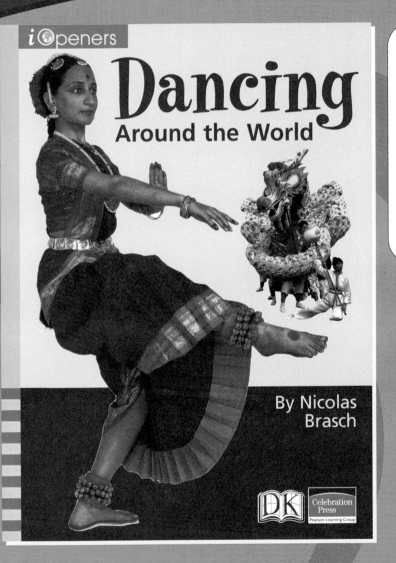

*i*Openers

Dancing
Around the World

By Nicolas Brasch

DK | Celebration Press
Pearson Learning Group

Words to Know

bow (p. 39): "to bend the upper part of the body in greeting"

bulging (p. 37): "sticking out"

fierce (p. 37): "wild or threatening"

rugby (p. 37): "a team sport similar to football"

Apply the Strategy

Lesson 1

Using Discussion to Clarify

1. Read pages 36–39.
2. Record words or ideas that you need to clarify in a list, labeling it *Things to Clarify*.
3. Work with a partner to clarify.

Things to Clarify

Lesson 2

Reading Ahead and Rereading to Clarify

1. Skim pages 36–39.
2. Record things you are confused about and your ideas for resolving them in a T-chart, labeling the left side *My Confusions* and the right side *How I Solve Them*.

My Confusions	How I Solve Them

Lesson 3

Activating Prior Knowledge to Clarify

1. Skim pages 36–39.
2. Record confusing concepts in a T-chart, labeling the left side *Things to Clarify* and the right side *Prior Knowledge*.
3. Work with a partner to discuss how your prior knowledge and experiences can help you resolve the confusion.

Things to Clarify	Prior Knowledge

Contents

Dancing Around the World

Start tapping your feet, and get ready to move. We are going dancing around the world. People dance for all sorts of reasons. They dance to celebrate an event or to entertain an audience. People tell stories and express emotions through dance. Sometimes people dance simply to enjoy themselves.

Let's take a closer look at a few dances. The dances come from many places. As you read, look for the different roles dance plays in different countries.

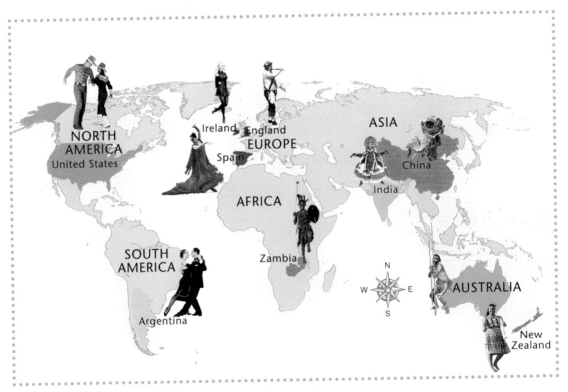

People do different dances throughout the world.

New Zealand Haka

Visitors to New Zealand are often greeted by a fierce sight. A line of men stand with their eyes bulging and tongues sticking out. They slap their chests, shake their hands, and yell. They are dancing the Haka, the traditional Maori welcome. The only music comes from the dancers' chanting as they move.

People seeing the Haka dance for the first time might find it scary. In fact, Maori warriors danced the Haka to prepare for battle. However, the Haka is most often danced to welcome visitors.

All Blacks Haka

The New Zealand rugby team is known as the All Blacks. The All Blacks perform the Haka before each game to challenge their opponents.

Maori men in traditional dress perform a welcoming Haka.

North America

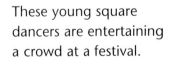

NORTH AMERICA
United States

The United States is located in North America.

Square Dancing of the United States

Swing your partner! **Promenade** right! We are going square dancing in the United States.

Square dancing is a type of country dancing. Country dancing came from the folk dances of English, Irish, and Scottish immigrants. These dance styles changed over time into the popular forms that are danced today. Square dancing is called a **social dance** because it brings people in the community together.

These young square dancers are entertaining a crowd at a festival.

Square Dancing Steps

left arm turn   cross hand swing   promenade

There are specific dance movements, or figures, in square dancing. First, groups of four couples form a square shape. Then a "caller" shouts out the figures in time to the music. The dancers follow the caller's instructions. Couples may take turns joining other couples and doing steps. They might bow to each other or turn in a circle.

Sometimes square dancing is done to lively **bluegrass** music. Bluegrass is traditionally played with stringed instruments, such as fiddles and banjos. Today, square dancing is also done to modern recorded music.

banjo

Summarizing and Synthesizing
Great Readers Make Sense of Text

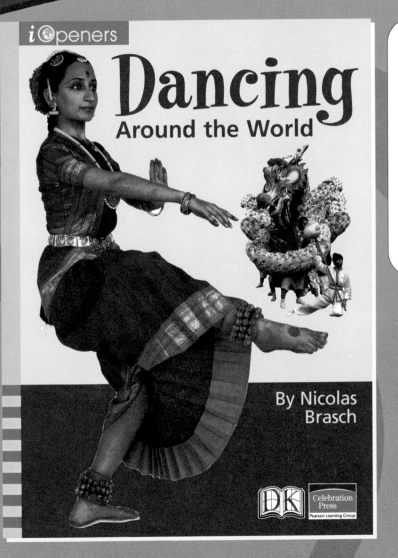

i◎peners

Dancing
Around the World

By Nicolas Brasch

DK Celebration Press
Pearson Learning Group

Apply the Strategy

Lesson 1

Pausing to Paraphrase as You Read

1. Read pages 42–43. Use sticky notes to mark the most important ideas, and pause after every few sentences to paraphrase what you have read.
2. Record your paraphrased sentences in a sequential list, labeling it *Kathakali Dance of India*.

Kathakali Dance of India

Lesson 2

Distinguishing Between Main Ideas and Details to Create a Summary

1. Read pages 44–45. Identify the main ideas and supporting details.
2. Discuss the main ideas with a partner and then write a short summary for the chapter.

Flamenco of Spain

Lesson 3

Combining Related Information

1. Skim pages 44–45. Record the main idea and related details in a summary web.
2. Discuss your summary web with a partner and then write a summary.

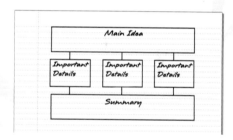

Main Idea

| Important Details | Important Details | Important Details |

Summary

Asia

Kathakali Dance of India

India and China are located in Asia.

Our journey begins in India, home of a dance called kathakali (KUT-uh-KUHL-ee). The word *kathakali* means "story-play." The dance began in the 1600s. Today, it is performed at theaters.

This dance tells stories through movement, expressions, and gestures. Kathakali dancers act out stories from two famous Indian poems, the *Ramayana* (ruh-MY-yuh-nuh) and the *Mahabharata* (MAH-huh-BAH-ruh-tuh). These poems tell of the struggle between good and evil.

Kathakali dance has musical **accompaniment**. The only instruments used are **percussion** instruments. These include cymbals, drums, and gongs.

Kathakali dancers wear elaborate costumes.

Kathakali makeup and costumes are colorful. Dancers playing evil characters wear green makeup. Those playing heroes paint their faces red or black. It often takes dancers many hours to put on their makeup since designs are so complicated.

Only men dance the kathakali. The dancers need to be strong and flexible. They work hard to train their bodies.

1 The dancer uses a stem from a coconut leaf to apply makeup.

The heavy headdress is called a kiritam.

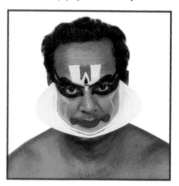

2 The dancer frames his face with white paper to make a chutti.

3 The dancer reddens the whites of his eyes.

Europe

Ireland
England
EUROPE
Spain

Spain, Ireland, and England are located in Europe.

Flamenco of Spain

Welcome to Spain, home to flamenco (fluh-MEHNG-koh) dance. Hundreds of years ago, a group of people called Romanies traveled from India to Spain. Their music and dance is called flamenco. Dancers use flamenco to express their feelings on both joyous and sad occasions.

Flamenco dancing is accompanied by singing called cante (KAHN-tay). The music is played on the guitar. Dancers sometimes use handheld percussion instruments called **castanets** as they dance.

castanets

Flamenco music is provided by the guitar. Until the 1800s, only singing accompanied the dancing.

Both men and women dance the flamenco.

Flamenco dancing focuses on the feet, arms, and hands. The dancers' feet are never still; they continuously pound the floor. This footwork is known as **zapateado** (zahp-ah-tay-AH-doh). The dancers turn their arms gracefully, sometimes reaching high above their heads. They clap their hands.

As the dance progresses, the dancers move faster and faster. For a moment, they don't seem to be aware of what is happening around them. This moment is called **duende** (DWEN-day), or the trance.

Women flamenco dancers usually wear long, frilly costumes.

Glossary

accompaniment	something that goes along with something else
accordion	an instrument with a keyboard on one side and a middle that expands and contracts
ballroom dancing	social dancing in which couples follow a pattern of steps
bandoneon	a type of accordion used in tango music
bluegrass	traditional style of music with stringed instruments, such as fiddles and banjos
castanets	handheld percussion instruments
clans	groups of people with a common ancestor, like families
didgeridoo	a musical instrument from Australia that is made from a hollowed-out log
duende	the trance flamenco dancers may experience
Indigenous	first inhabitants of an area
martial arts	forms of self-defense, such as karate or kung fu
percussion	instruments that produce a sound after being struck
promenade	dance step in square dancing where a couple marches together in a circle
social dance	dance that brings people in the community together
uillean pipes	an Irish instrument made of a bag, bellows, and pipes
zapateado	the footwork in flamenco dancing

When the Earth Shakes

By Charles Higgins and Regina Higgins

Words to Know

jolt (p. 62): "to move in a jerky manner"

slabs (p. 54): "thick, flat pieces"

spouted (p. 53): "shot out with force"

tremors (p. 54): "shaking or trembling"

Apply the Strategy

Thinking About What You Know Before Reading

1. Look at the cover of *When the Earth Shakes* on page 48. Think about what you know about earthquakes.
2. Record your ideas on a concept web.

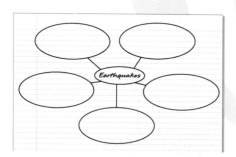

Considering Your Purpose for Reading

1. Look at the contents page on page 52. Think about the reasons someone might have for reading this book.
2. Record your purposes for reading and your background knowledge in a T-chart, labeling the left side *My Purpose for Reading* and the right side *What I Know*.

My Purpose for Reading	What I Know

Previewing to Activate Background Knowledge

1. Preview pages 52–78. Use the information you gather to narrow down the background knowledge you'll need to understand the text.
2. Modify your concept web from Lesson 1.
3. Discuss your changes with a partner.

When the
Earth Shakes

By Charles Higgins and Regina Higgins

Words to Know

damage (p. 71): "loss or harm caused by an injury to a person or property"

extended (p. 71): "reached across a distance"

withstand (p. 64): "to stand against"

Apply the Strategy

Lesson 1

Activating Background Knowledge Throughout Reading

1. Read pages 53–70. Use what you know about the topic to make connections to the text.
2. Record your new ideas about the topic in a concept web.

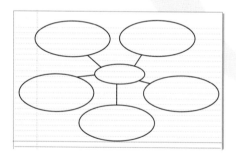

Lesson 2

Asking Questions to Fill Gaps in Your Background Knowledge

1. Skim pages 53–70. Mark places in the text where you feel you need more information to understand the text.

2. Record what you know, gaps in your background knowledge, and the answers you find on a K-W-L chart. Label the columns *What I Know, What I Want to Learn,* and *What I Learned.*

What I Know	What I Want to Learn	What I Learned

Lesson 3

Revising Background Knowledge to Accommodate New Information

1. Read pages 71–78. Think about how some of the new information may cause you to change what you think. Revise your concept web or K-W-L chart to reflect your revised or new background knowledge.
2. Change your web or chart by adding new information and crossing off any information that you no longer need.

Contents

Chapter 1

It's an Earthquake!

A woman and her children watched as the water in their swimming pool suddenly spouted five feet in the air. A man watched cars in a parking lot hop around as if they were toys. A woman went to sleep with her bed against one wall in her bedroom. The bed was against another wall when she woke up.

A parking lot and building are destroyed by an earthquake.

A boy and his dad were in their car. It suddenly started to bounce, as if there were big bumps in the road. The road itself bent and twisted. The broken concrete slabs dipped and rolled like the waves of an ocean.

These people were experiencing earthquakes. An earthquake is a sudden shaking of the earth's surface. The tremors can be so mild that they barely make leaves on a tree flutter. They can be so violent that they cause cracks in the earth hundreds of miles long.

Damage from the 1994 Los Angeles earthquake

Rescuers look for people after an earthquake in San Francisco.

Major earthquakes can cause great destruction. The most serious problems happen when buildings collapse. People inside can be trapped.

After an earthquake is over, the danger and damage may still go on. The water in damaged pipes below the street may burst out like a fountain. Whole sections of a city may be flooded. The roads and streets themselves may crack open. When that happens emergency crews cannot reach people who need help.

When gas pipelines under the street break, the leaking gas can start fires. If water pipes are broken, firefighters may be unable to get water to put out the flames.

Cities are not the only places damaged by earthquakes. In hilly areas, loose rock and soil tumble down hillsides when the ground shakes. The landslide becomes a mudslide if the ground has been soaked by rain.

In areas with lots of snow, the shaking ground causes snow and ice to roll down hillsides. Like a landslide or mudslide, an avalanche crushes everything it reaches.

After an earthquake, a landslide
caused more damage to this house.

Sometimes a small earthquake can cause more damage than a large one. It depends on where the earthquake happens. This makes comparing the size of earthquakes difficult.

The Richter scale is the system most people use to compare earthquakes. This scale tells how much the ground shakes at any point 60 miles away from the epicenter of the earthquake. The epicenter is the point in the ground where the earthquake starts.

The Richter scale goes from 1 to 9. The number 1 means an earthquake too small for people to feel. The number 9 is the strongest earthquake. Each step on the Richter scale is for an earthquake ten times stronger than the last step. So an earthquake measuring 7 is ten times stronger than one registering 6. Scientists measure the movements of the ground with an instrument called a seismograph. How much the ground moves is shown on a computer or on paper as jagged lines that go up and down. A strong earthquake will be recorded with big jagged lines.

It usually takes an earthquake registering between 5 and 6 to damage homes. Major earthquakes are any that measure over 7. An earthquake that measures as high as 8 on the Richter scale is rare. There has never been an earthquake recorded as high as 9.

About 500,000 or more earthquakes happen every year around the world. Most of these earthquakes are very small. About 5,000 of the earthquakes are big enough for people to feel. About 1,000 of them are strong enough to cause some damage.

Anchorage, Alaska, after the 1964 earthquake

~~~~Earthshaking Fact~~~~

The longest earthquake on record lasted four minutes. The earthquake shook Alaska in March of 1964. It was also the strongest earthquake ever recorded. It measured between 8 and 9 on the Richter scale.

Chapter 2

How Earthquakes Happen

In ancient times, many people made up myths, or stories, to explain why the earth shakes. Native Americans living in California told the tale of six turtles who supported the world on their backs. The Great Spirit told the turtles not to move. When the turtles argued, they tried to move away from each other. The earth shook when they moved.

Rock drawing of a turtle

People in California and all over the world now know that earthquakes are caused by movements within the earth. These powerful movements come from deep within the earth. They travel upward to the earth's surface where people can feel them. To understand how these movements shake the earth's surface, think of the earth as having several layers instead of being a solid ball.

Earth's tectonic plates

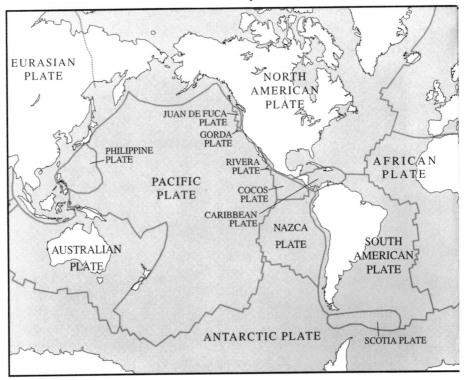

The outer layer, or crust, is hard and rocky. It is like a shell that is about 70 miles thick. Unlike a shell, though, the crust is not smooth. It is in pieces that fit together like a jigsaw puzzle. These pieces are called tectonic plates. Every ocean and continent lies on a tectonic plate that is part of the earth's crust.

The earth's crust rests on another layer. It is called the mantle, which is a mass of partly melted rock. The melted rock is called magma. It is soft, gooey, and very hot. As the magma moves, the tectonic plates move, too.

The plates on the mantle move very, very slowly. The plate that holds North America and the plate that holds Europe, for example, are moving apart at the rate of four inches per year. This is too slow for people to see or feel.

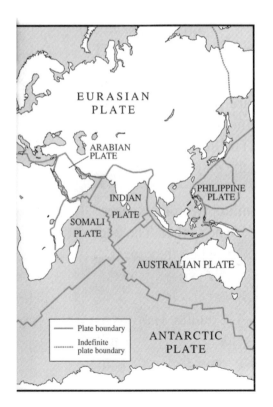

EURASIAN PLATE

ARABIAN PLATE

INDIAN PLATE

PHILIPPINE PLATE

SOMALI PLATE

AUSTRALIAN PLATE

Plate boundary
Indefinite plate boundary

ANTARCTIC PLATE

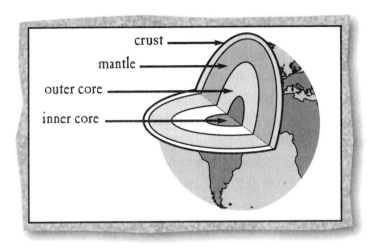

The layers of the earth

Beneath the mantle lies the outer core. At the very center is the inner core, a ball of solid rock. The inner and outer cores are very hot. Scientists think that temperatures in the inner core may reach 9,000 degrees Fahrenheit. The heat from the core acts like a furnace to keep the magma soft and constantly moving.

The plates move easily unless two plates meet and try to push past or under each other. The edges of the plates can stick together when they meet. The magma underneath the plates keeps moving. This forces the plates together even harder.

The plates can stay stuck for hundreds or even thousands of years. Then suddenly, the plates jolt past each other. This movement of the earth's crust causes an earthquake.

After the first sudden movement, the plates may move a little more. These later movements cause more shaking and are called aftershocks. Aftershocks can occur hours, days, weeks, or even months after the first big earthquake. Usually, the later the aftershocks come, the smaller they are.

The point under the ground where the plates shift is called the focus. The focus can be more than 400 miles below the earth's surface. This is where the earthquake begins and where its force is the most powerful.

The vibrations that start at the focus move upward at a rate of up to ten miles per second. The spot above the focus on the earth's surface is the epicenter. The most destruction happens at the epicenter during an earthquake.

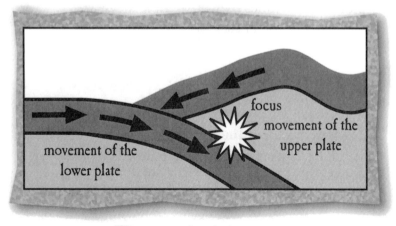

Where an earthquake happens

After an earthquake in Mexico City

There are places on Earth that are much more likely than others to have major earthquakes. These places sit above the point where the edges of tectonic plates meet. Skyscrapers, homes, highways, and even sports arenas have all been built in such places. Sometimes they are built to withstand an earthquake. Sometimes they are not.

Earthshaking Fact

In 1985 a powerful earthquake knocked down buildings in Mexico City. The epicenter was more than 200 miles away!

Chapter 3

Living on the Edge

In the afternoon of October 17, 1989, baseball fans filled San Francisco's Candlestick Park. They were excited for the start of the third game of the World Series between the San Francisco Giants and the Oakland Athletics.

Suddenly, there was a rumbling across the field. The bleachers shook. Blocks of concrete fell from

the stadium's balconies. San Francisco was having an earthquake!

Players help people after the earthquake in Candlestick Park.

Collapsed highway in San Francisco, 1989

Amazingly, no one in Candlestick Park was seriously hurt by the earthquake. The worst damage was in West Oakland across San Francisco Bay.

The earthquake struck at 5:04 P.M. The roadways were packed with cars. One highway fell on top of another. Many people were trapped in their cars, and some died.

The 1989 earthquake measured 6.4 on the Richter scale. This was not the first time San Francisco had experienced an earthquake. The same area had suffered a bigger, more serious earthquake 83 years earlier.

Early one April morning in 1906, a terrible earthquake shook San Francisco. It measured 7.7 on the Richter scale. Buildings tumbled into rubble in less than two minutes. The streets cracked open. People fled their houses in a panic. Many others were trapped in the fallen buildings.

The damage that came after the earthquake was even worse. Gas lamps and stoves caused fires when they fell over. Underground gas pipes also burst. Fire spread all over the city. It took three days to put out all the fires. Over 28,000 buildings burned to the ground. The earthquake and its fires killed nearly 2,500 people.

After the San Francisco earthquake in 1906

San Francisco's two major earthquakes were not unusual for that part of the country. California has more earthquakes than any other part of the United States. This is because San Francisco lies just at the meeting point of two tectonic plates. These are the Pacific Plate and the North American Plate.

The San Andreas Fault in California

As seen from above, the San Andreas Fault looks like
a large crack in the ground.

Where the plates meet is called the San Andreas
Fault. A fault is a crack in the earth's surface,
usually between two tectonic plates. The San
Andreas Fault runs nearly the whole length of
California. It passes under San Francisco and very
near Los Angeles. The San Andreas Fault causes
many of the earthquakes in California.

There are also smaller fault lines in California.
After the 1987 earthquake in Los Angeles,
scientists discovered six fault lines under the city.
Any of these faults, together with the San Andreas
Fault, can cause an earthquake.

The entire coast around the Pacific Ocean, including California, has many earthquakes. Look back at the map on page 60. This area includes the Pacific Plate, the Nazca Plate, and the Australian Plate. The coasts of North and South America, Japan, and islands in the western Pacific are also in this region. About three out of four earthquakes in the world occur here.

Earthshaking Fact

One California fault is the San Gabriel Fault. It lies in the area in which Native Americans long ago told stories about the earth trembling when the turtles argued. Earthquakes must have happened often there.

Chapter 4

Tsunamis and Volcanoes

One of the strongest earthquakes ever recorded began in Chile and rumbled all around the Pacific Ocean in May of 1960. Damage extended from Chile to California, Alaska, Hawaii, and even Japan.

The fault running along the coast of Chile moved in several jolts. The largest earthquake measured 8.3 on the Richter scale. Aftershocks caused more earthquakes within hours.

Damage in a Japanese harbor in 1960 after an earthquake caused large ocean waves

Valdivia, Chile, is built on a fault. The city trembled and sank almost seven feet as the tectonic plate jolted into a new position. The earthquakes caused rock slides in Chile's Andes Mountains. Two days after the first earthquake, a volcano erupted from one of the mountains. Burning lava poured down the mountainside.

Volcano in Chile

Damage after a tsunami in Hawaii

After the earthquakes, ocean waves grew enormous in places all around the Pacific Ocean. These waves are called tsunamis (soo NAHM eez). They flooded areas of the Hawaiian Islands 20 feet deep. The waves that hit the shore crushed buildings. Many homes, cars, and heavy machinery were washed away. In Japan, waves surged 20 feet inland. In California, waves reached more than 250 feet inland in one spot.

How could there be earthquakes, enormous ocean waves, and volcanoes all happening at the same time? The same movements in the earth's crust that cause earthquakes can cause volcanoes and tsunamis, too.

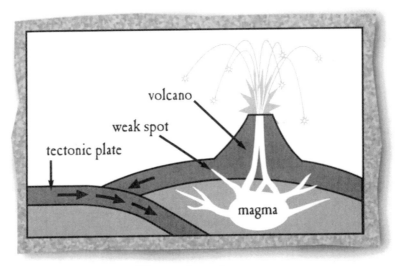

How a volcano forms

Most volcanoes in the world are located along the same fault lines where earthquakes happen, especially in the countries around the Pacific Ocean. That's why this area is often called the Ring of Fire.

A fault line between tectonic plates creates a lot of weak spots in the crust. The hot, liquid magma under the earth's crust seeps into these cracks or weak spots. The magma can push the crust up in a point, forming a volcanic mountain. The formation of this mountain can take hundreds or even thousands of years.

The magma is mixed with explosive bubbly gases. So, when the magma finally breaks through the mountain, it often explodes. The fiery magma shoots out of the mountaintop, spraying red-hot liquid and rock all around. A volcano is born!

When magma pours out onto the earth's surface, it is called lava. Lava is fiery hot. The lava that pours down a volcano's mountainsides burns everything in its path.

The tiny bits of lava that shoot up in an explosion cool as they hit the air, like sparks from a campfire. As the bits fall, they cover the ground and everything else with volcanic ash.

A man washes volcanic ash from a car after the eruption of Mount St. Helens in Washington in 1980

Volcanoes can also create new land. Volcanoes form and erupt where plates are spreading apart. Lava from the underwater volcanoes fills in the crack between the spreading plates. This is happening in the Atlantic Ocean.

The Hawaiian Islands in the Pacific Ocean were formed by volcanoes in a different way. One hot spot of magma in the earth's mantle pushed magma up through the crust. This action formed a volcano that poked above the water. The crust moved very slowly over the hot spot. A line of volcanic islands formed as the crust moved.

The Hawaiian Islands were formed by volcanoes long ago.

Damage after an earthquake and tsunami in Japan in 1993

Tsunamis are formed when an earthquake happens on the ocean floor. The powerful tremors shake the water in the same way that an earthquake on land shakes the surrounding area.

Small waves begin to form on the surface as the water shakes. The waves get larger and larger as the shaking continues. Some tsunamis tower nearly 100 feet high by the time they reach land. These powerful waves can also be hundreds of miles wide.

Tsunamis travel quickly and can hit a coast suddenly. They can move at a speed of 500 miles per hour. This is as fast as a jet plane. Waves may repeatedly pound the shore for hours. They knock down buildings, rip up beaches, and flood the whole area.

Japan is one country that has been hit by many tsunamis and earthquakes. The Japanese have learned from their experience with these monster waves and earthquakes. They are becoming experts at rescuing people trapped by floods, in crumbled buildings, and by fallen rock.

Earthshaking Fact

Tsunami is a Japanese word meaning "harbor wave." The island of Japan has been hit by at least 15 tsunamis in the past 300 years.

Gloria Estefan

Book Treks   By Lou Ann Walker

Words to Know

audience (p. 83): "a group that listens or watches"

fled (p. 85) "ran away from"

patience (p. 89): "being able to put up with hardships, pain, or delay calmly and without anger"

Apply the Strategy

Lesson 1

Making Text-to-Self Connections

1. Read pages 83–90. Think about how the events and people in the text relate to your own life.
2. Record your text-to-self connections in a T-chart, labeling the left side *My Text-to-Self Connection* and the right side *How It Helps Me Understand the Text*.

My Text-to-Self Connection	How It Helps Me Understand the Text

Lesson 2

Making Text-to-Text Connections

1. Skim pages 83–90. Think about ways the text reminds you of other texts you've read.
2. Record your text-to-text connections in a three-column chart, labeling the columns *Other Text I've Read, My Connection,* and *How It Helps Me Understand the Text.*

Other Text I've Read	My Connection	How It Helps Me Understand the Text

Lesson 3

Making Text-to-World Connections

1. Skim pages 83–90. Think about how the text links to places or things you know about, but haven't experienced.
2. Record your text-to-world connections in a T-chart, labeling the left side *My Text-to-World Connection* and the right side *How It Helps Me Understand the Text.*

My Text-to-World Connection	How It Helps Me Understand the Text

Contents

Gloria Live!

Bright lights flash as the audience cheers. Gloria Estefan, wearing a glittering gown, joyfully dances and sings her way across the stage. The air crackles with electricity. "Turn the beat around!" she sings, and the audience goes crazy.

Gloria Estefan performing

Gloria Estefan is a music superstar who has sold more than 70 million records. Her songs mix pop, rock, and Latin **rhythms**. Gloria has won several Grammy awards for her music.

Gloria began her career singing hits in the Spanish language. When she started singing in English, her songs rose to the top of the English-language charts.

An artist who can reach different audiences is called a **crossover** artist. Gloria is a good example. In fact, together with her husband, Emilio, she has helped other stars to cross over as well.

All the while, she has put her family first in her life. She even takes them along when she tours.

Gloria battled many problems before and after she became famous. There was even an accident that could have ended her career. Here is her story.

Gloria's Family Flees Cuba

Gloria Fajardo was born in Havana, Cuba, on September 1, 1957. In 1959, the government of Cuba changed, and people who did not like the new leader of Cuba fled the country. Gloria's family was among those people. The Fajardos left Cuba and settled in Miami, Florida.

The island of Cuba lies near the southern tip of Florida.

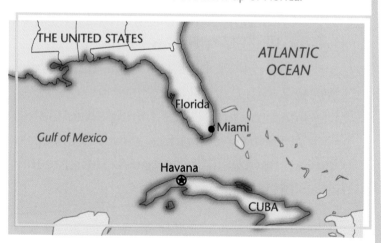

85

José Fajardo, Gloria's father, went back to Cuba to try to help the old government leaders return to power. He was caught and put into prison. It was up to Gloria's mother, also named Gloria, to find a home for her family.

There were many Cubans in Miami, and some, including the Fajardos, experienced **prejudice**. The Fajardo family had trouble finding an apartment. **Landlords** put up signs that read, "No children, no pets, and no Cubans."

No matter how difficult things were, Gloria's mother, "Mami," always took time to sing her daughter to sleep. Little Glorita, as Gloria was called, loved to hear Mami's voice.

In 1962, Mr. Fajardo returned to America and joined the army. The family lived on many army bases. Gloria's sister, Rebecca, was born at a base in Texas in 1964. Shortly after that, Gloria's father went to fight in the Vietnam War.

As an adult, Gloria returned to visit one of the army bases where she lived as a child.

While her father was away in Vietnam, Gloria began sending him tapes of her singing. He wrote back to her, "One day, you're going to be a great star." Many mothers and fathers say such hopeful words to their children, but few parents have their wishes come true in such a big way.

One Country, Two Cultures

Gloria loved listening to American rock music on the radio. She felt she was part of two **cultures**. She was an American, but she was also a Cuban. Often, she was the only person in her class who spoke both English and Spanish.

An outdoor scene in Havana, Cuba, the city Gloria left when she was two.

Sadly, Gloria's father became ill soon after he came back from the war in 1968. He had a disease called multiple sclerosis. Over time, he lost the use of his legs and needed a wheelchair.

Mrs. Fajardo had been a teacher in Cuba. In America, she worked days and took classes at night. She wanted to open a school.

Although the family faced problems, Gloria's parents were very loving. The young girl learned important lessons. She admired her mother's hard work and strength. Mami also kept Cuban culture alive in their home.

Gloria was a shy child who liked to write poetry. She had very little social life, because she had to look after her younger sister and her father. "Taking care of him taught me patience," Gloria said.

When life seemed tough, Gloria refused to cry. Instead, she would go to her room to sing and play her guitar.

Gloria has said about this time of her life, "Music was the only way I had to just let go. So I sang for fun."

In 1975, when Gloria was 17, she met Emilio Estefan. Emilio played the keyboard for a band named the Miami Latin Boys. He would help Gloria take the first steps to fame.

Gloria and Emilio

Glossary

charity a fund or group that helps people who are in need

crossover in the music business, being popular with more than one group of listeners

cultures the beliefs and customs of a certain group of people

determined to make up one's mind very firmly

landlords people who rent out buildings or apartments

paralyzed having lost part or all of the power to move or feel in a part of the body

physical therapists people who are trained to help others regain physical movement after an illness or injury

prejudice having a dislike or distrust of people because of their race, religion, or country

rhythms the natural beat in some music

Making Inferences
Great Readers Use What They Know

When the Earth Shakes

By Charles Higgins and Regina Higgins

Apply the Strategy

Lesson 1

Using What You Know to Make Inferences

1. Read pages 95–96. Use what you know and clues you find in the text to make inferences.
2. Record inferences in a three-column chart, labeling the columns *Text Clues*, *Background Knowledge*, and *My Inferences.*

Text Clues	Background Knowledge	My Inference

Lesson 2

Using Inferences to Clarify Words and Concepts

1. Read pages 97–99. Think about how using inferences can help you clarify text that you find confusing.
2. Record your inferences in a three-column chart, labeling the columns *What Confuses Me, Clues That Help Me Make an Inference,* and *My Inference.*

What Confuses Me	Clues That Help Me Make an Inference	My Inference

Lesson 3

Revising and Expanding Inferences as You Read

1. Skim pages 95–99. Review the charts you created in Lesson 1 and 2. Think about your inferences and how you might revise or expand on them.
2. Record your revised or expanded inferences in a three-column chart, labeling the columns *My Inference, New Information,* and *My Revised/Expanded Inference.*

My Inference	New Information	My Revised / Expanded Inference

Contents

Chapter 5

Earthquake Rescues

People rush to try to help others who are hurt or trapped in collapsed buildings after an earthquake or tsunami hits. They have to be careful. The possibility of aftershocks means the possibility of more damage. Loose parts of buildings may fall. Only specially trained rescue workers may go into damaged areas. This work is very dangerous, but it is the only way to save people's lives.

Japanese rescue workers check for survivors.

Rescuers look for earthquake survivors at the Kobe train station.

Trained rescuers travel around the world to help where earthquakes and other disasters have occurred. The American Rescue Team International, ARTI, has been at most major disasters since 1985.

A major earthquake in 1995 hit Kobe, one of Japan's largest cities. ARTI was there. This earthquake registered 7.2 on the Richter scale and lasted only 20 seconds. The damage was the worst Japan had seen in over 70 years. Nearly 180,000 buildings collapsed or were badly damaged.

The train station in Kobe collapsed with people inside. The ARTI rescuers crawled into spaces with as little as one-and-a-half feet of headroom. Sometimes they had to crawl like this for hundreds of feet, looking for survivors.

Rescuers also use special equipment to help find people trapped in buildings or by fallen rock. A trapped-person detector is a sensitive machine that can pick up small vibrations. When trapped people try to move, they shake the rubble or broken bits of building or rock that lie around them. The small vibrations caused by this movement travel through the rubble.

The detector picks up the noise of any slight vibration. It makes the noise much louder electronically. A person's breathing can be detected. Rescuers wear headphones to hear the sounds of people that they could not hear otherwise.

A rescuer uses a trapped-person detector.

A rescue dog and its handler search earthquake rubble.

Where people cannot go into collapsed buildings, specially trained dogs often can. Dogs are excellent rescue animals. They have a keen sense of smell. They can sniff to find people who are trapped without being able to see or hear them.

Dogs have another advantage over people as rescuers. They weigh less than people. This means they can walk on rubble that might collapse if a heavier person walked on it.

A dog is trained to bark loudly when it smells a person. Then the rescue people know where they have to go to get a person out.

There is a lot of work to be done to help people who have been rescued from an earthquake or any other disaster. Many people no longer have homes, food, or water. Several organizations from around the world, such as the Red Cross, help these people. They bring people medical care, food and water, and help in the rebuilding of homes.

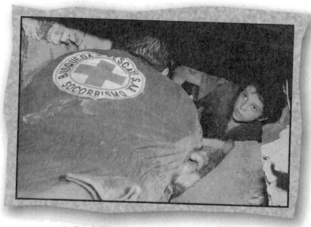

A Red Cross worker rescues a boy.

Earthshaking Fact

Douglas Copp is the director of ARTI. He has crawled through more than 800 collapsed buildings searching for trapped people. He has risked his life to save many others.

Glossary

absorb	[ub ZORB] to take in and not reflect or throw back
avalanche	[AV uh lanch] large mass of snow, ice, or rocks that slides swiftly down a mountain
calculate	[KAL kyoo layt] to determine; to find out, often by using mathematics
destruction	[dihs TRUK shun] the act of breaking up, tearing down, ruining, or spoiling
focus	[FOH kus] a center of activity; the point where rays of sound, movement, heat, or light come together or a point from which they spread
rubble	[RUB ul] broken pieces from damaged buildings
scale	[skayl] a series of marks along a line, with regular spaces in between, used for measuring; a series of steps based on size or amount
surged	[surjd] moved in a sudden strong rush
tectonic	[tek TAHN ihk] relating to or caused by a break or shape in the earth's crust
vibrations	[vye BRAY shunz] rapid movements back and forth